DISASTERS IN HISTORY

Shackleton
and the Lost Antarctic Expedition

by B. A. Hoena

illustrated by Dave Hoover
and Charles Barnett III

Consultant:

Robert Headland

Archivist and Curator

Scott Polar Research Institute

University of Cambridge, United Kingdom

Capstone
press

Mankato, Minnesota

Graphic Library is published by Capstone Press,
1710 Roe Crest Drive, North Mankato, Minnesota 56003.
www.capstonepub.com

Library of Congress Cataloging-in-Publication Data
Hoena, B. A.
Shackleton and the lost Antarctic expedition / by B. A. Hoena; illustrated by Dave Hoover and Charles Barnett III.
p. cm.—(Graphic library. Disasters in history)
Includes bibliographical references.
ISBN-13: 978-0-7368-5482-5 (hardcover)
ISBN-10: 0-7368-5482-7 (hardcover)
ISBN-13: 978-0-7368-6877-8 (softcover pbk.)
ISBN-10: 0-7368-6877-1 (softcover pbk.)
1. Shackleton, Ernest Henry, Sir, 1874–1922—Travel—Antarctica—Juvenile literature. 2. Imperial Trans-Antarctic Expedition (1914–1917)—Juvenile literature. 3. Antarctica—Discovery and exploration—British—Juvenile literature. 4. Endurance (Ship)—Juvenile literature. I. Hoover, Dave, 1955– ill. II. Barnett, Charles, III, ill. III. Title. IV. Series.
G850 1914 .S53 H63 2006
919.8'904—dc22 2005029848

Summary: In graphic novel format, tells the story of Antarctic explorer Ernest Shackleton and his failed attempt to cross the coldest and windiest continent on earth.

Art Direction and Design
Jason Knudson

Storyboard Artist
B. A. Hoena

Production Designer
Alison Thiele

Colorist
Benjamin Hunzeker

Editor
Erika L. Shores

Editor's note: Direct quotations from primary sources are indicated by a yellow background.

Direct quotations appear on the following pages:
Pages 6, 10, from crewmembers' diaries as quoted in *Endurance: Shackleton's Incredible Voyage* by Alfred Lansing, (Wheaton, Ill.: Tyndale House, 1999).
Pages 12, 15 (bottom), 21, from crewmembers' diaries and letters as quoted in *The* Endurance*: Shackleton's Legendary Antarctic Expedition* by Caroline Alexander, (New York: Alfred E. Knopf, 1998).
Pages 15 (top), 26, 27, from *South: A Memoir of the* Endurance *Voyage* by Ernest Shackleton, (New York: Carroll & Graf, 1998).

Printed in the United States 5946

Table of Contents

Chapter 1

A Daring Expedition

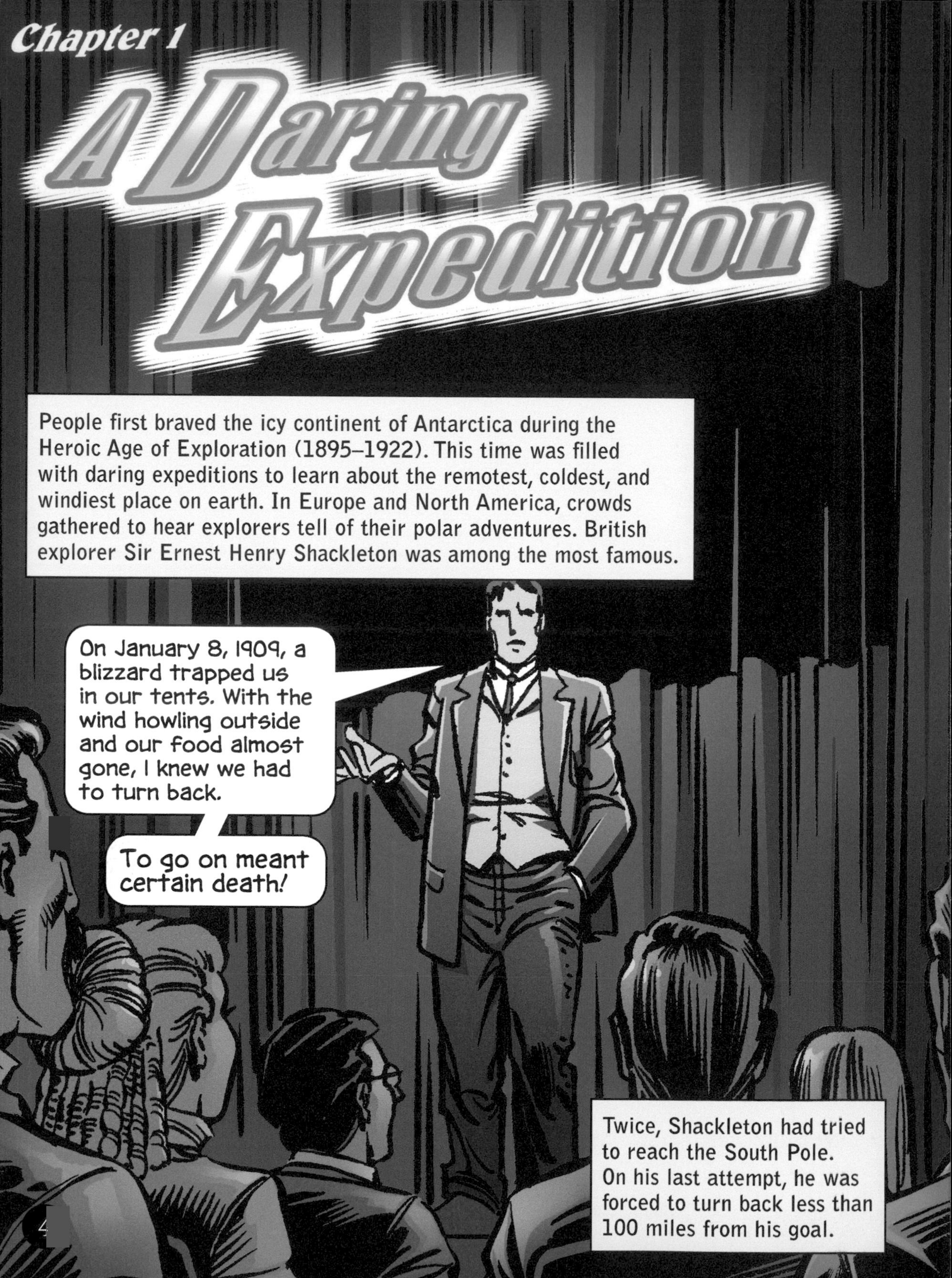
People first braved the icy continent of Antarctica during the Heroic Age of Exploration (1895–1922). This time was filled with daring expeditions to learn about the remotest, coldest, and windiest place on earth. In Europe and North America, crowds gathered to hear explorers tell of their polar adventures. British explorer Sir Ernest Henry Shackleton was among the most famous.
On January 8, 1909, a blizzard trapped us in our tents. With the wind howling outside and our food almost gone, I knew we had to turn back.
To go on meant certain death!
Twice, Shackleton had tried to reach the South Pole. On his last attempt, he was forced to turn back less than 100 miles from his goal.

Thank you!
Sir, you have a telegram.
Shackleton enjoyed his fame. But in the spring of 1912, he received news that changed everything.
Roald Amundsen reached the South Pole last December, on the 14th.
My dream—he has beaten me to it.
Shackleton knew people would now be more interested in the Norwegian explorer's successful journey than in his failed attempts.

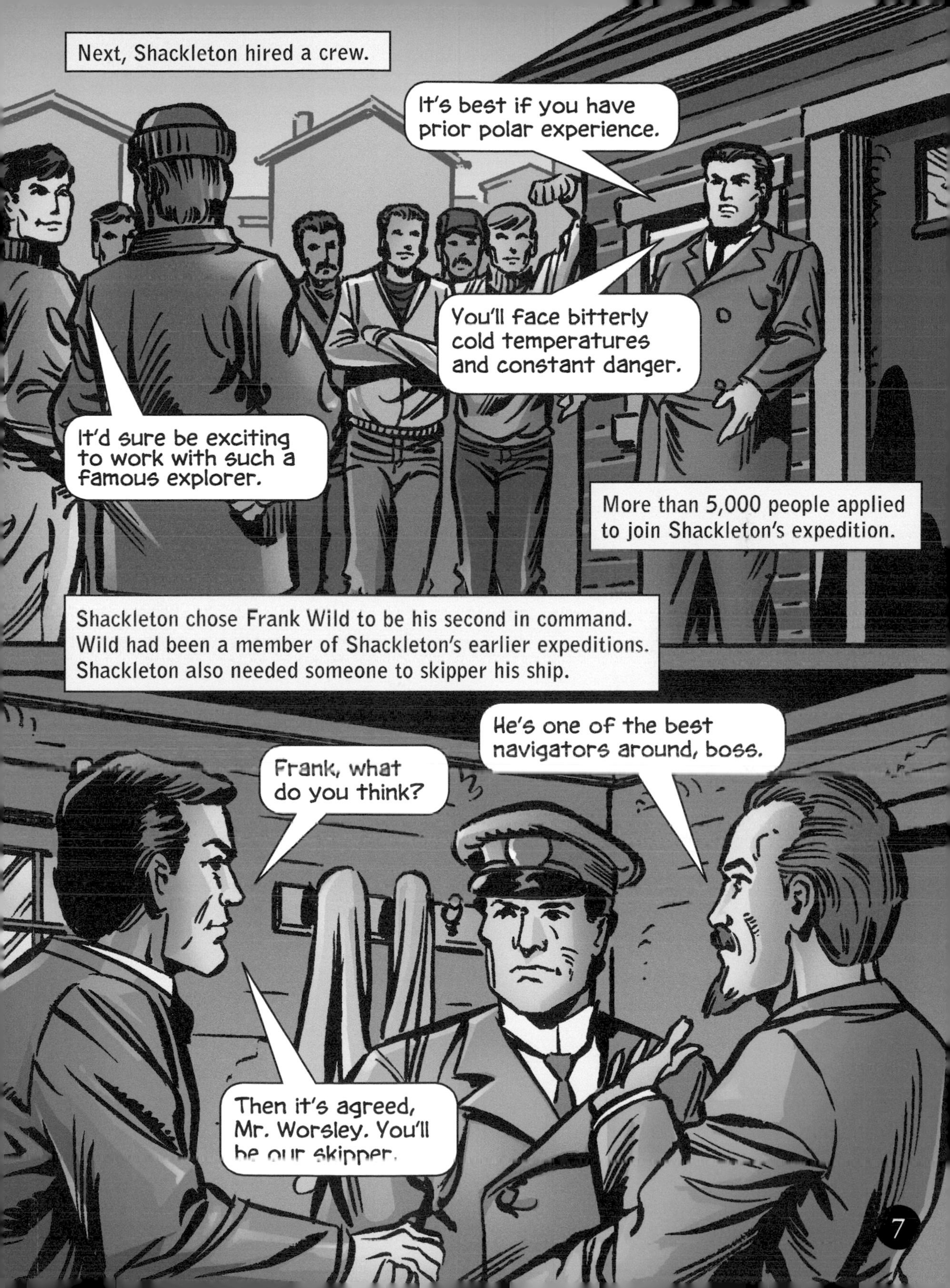
Next, Shackleton hired a crew.
It's best if you have prior polar experience.
You'll face bitterly cold temperatures and constant danger.
It'd sure be exciting to work with such a famous explorer.
More than 5,000 people applied to join Shackleton's expedition.
Shackleton chose Frank Wild to be his second in command. Wild had been a member of Shackleton's earlier expeditions. Shackleton also needed someone to skipper his ship.
Frank, what do you think?
He's one of the best navigators around, boss.
Then it's agreed, Mr. Worsley. You'll be our skipper.

Chapter 2

Locked in Ice

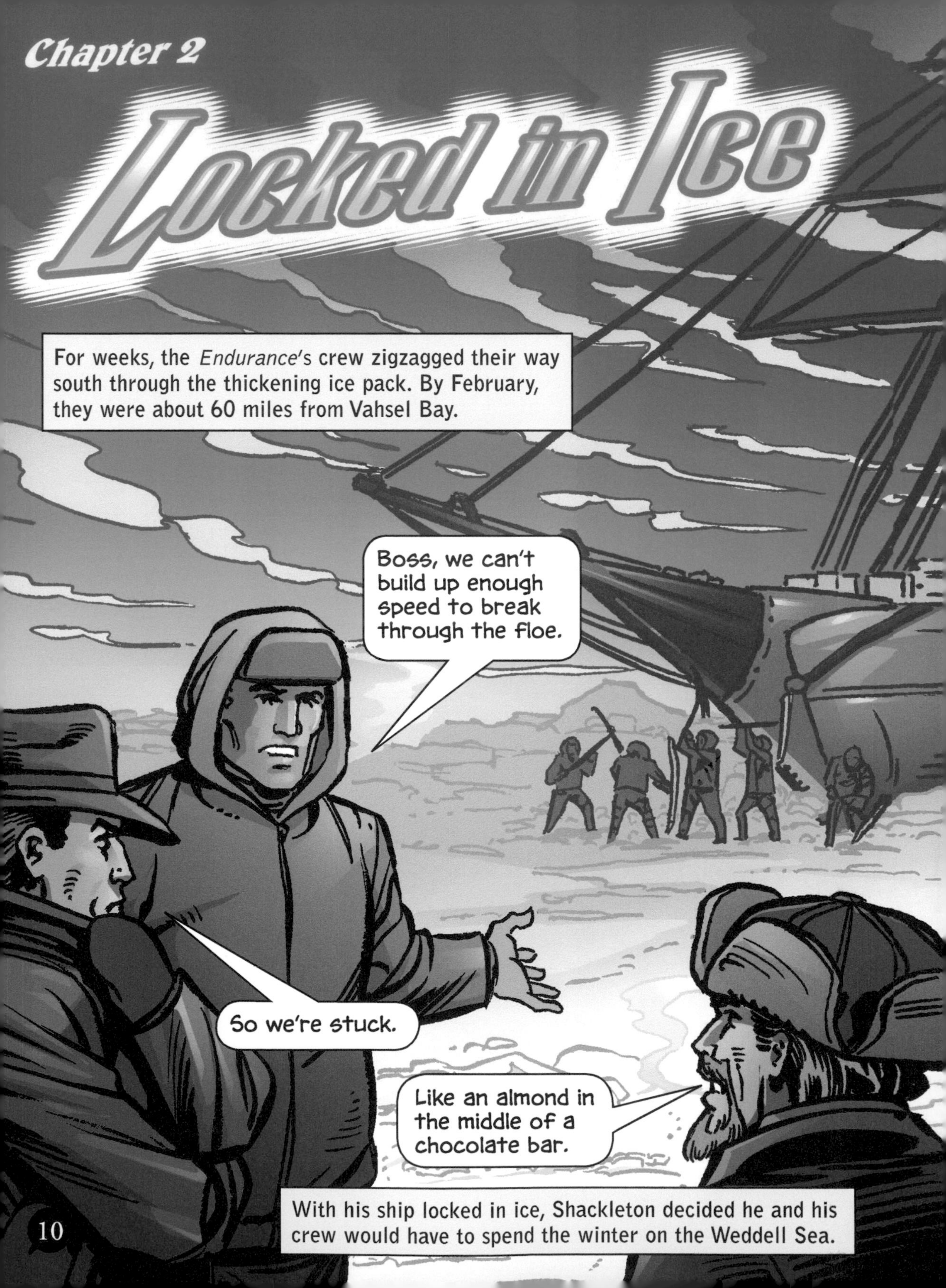

For weeks, the *Endurance*'s crew zigzagged their way south through the thickening ice pack. By February, they were about 60 miles from Vahsel Bay.
Boss, we can't build up enough speed to break through the floe.
So we're stuck.
Like an almond in the middle of a chocolate bar.
With his ship locked in ice, Shackleton decided he and his crew would have to spend the winter on the Weddell Sea.

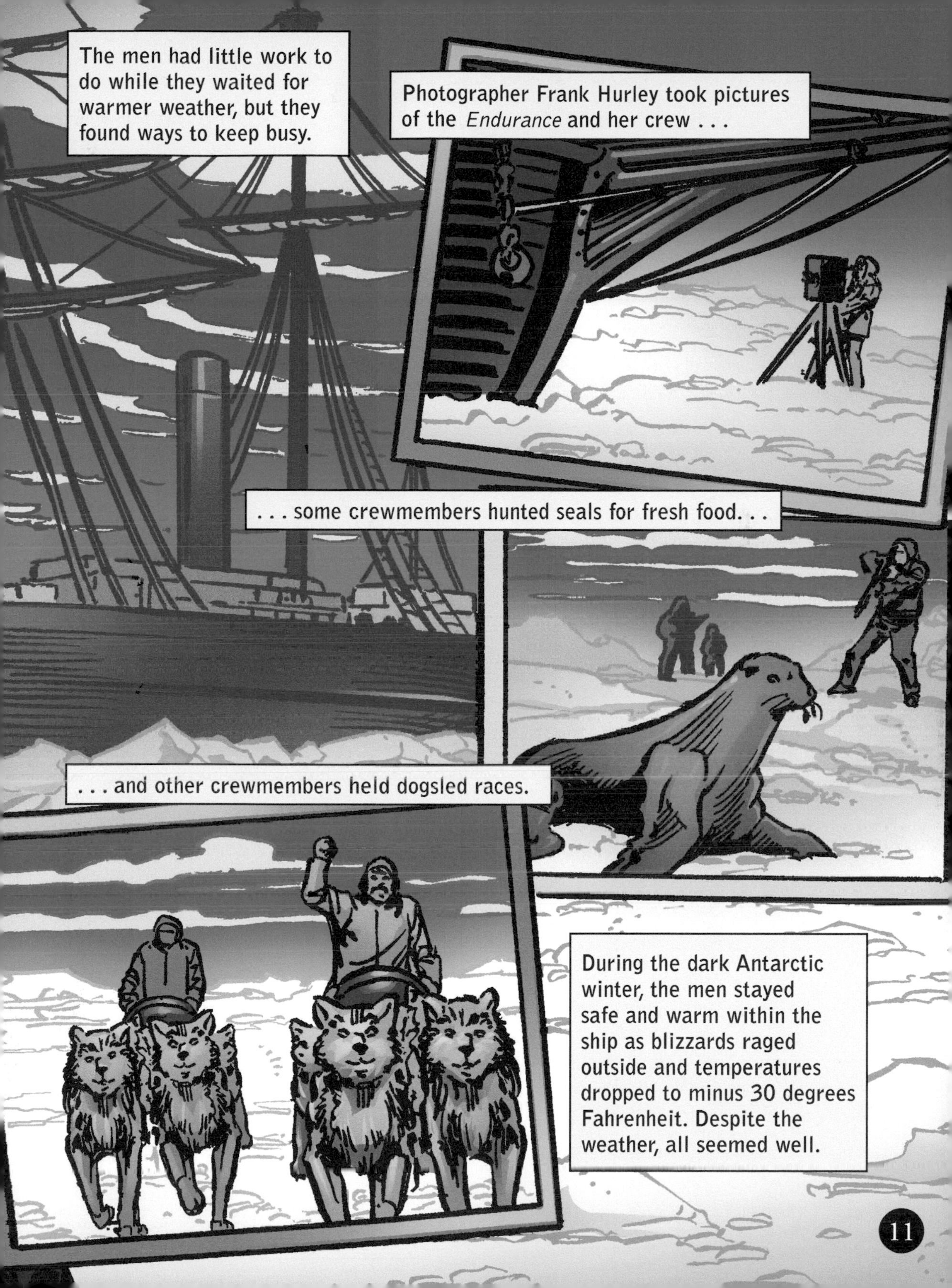
The men had little work to do while they waited for warmer weather, but they found ways to keep busy.
Photographer Frank Hurley took pictures of the *Endurance* and her crew . . .
. . . some crewmembers hunted seals for fresh food. . .
. . . and other crewmembers held dogsled races.
During the dark Antarctic winter, the men stayed safe and warm within the ship as blizzards raged outside and temperatures dropped to minus 30 degrees Fahrenheit. Despite the weather, all seemed well.

Chapter 3 The Fight to Survive

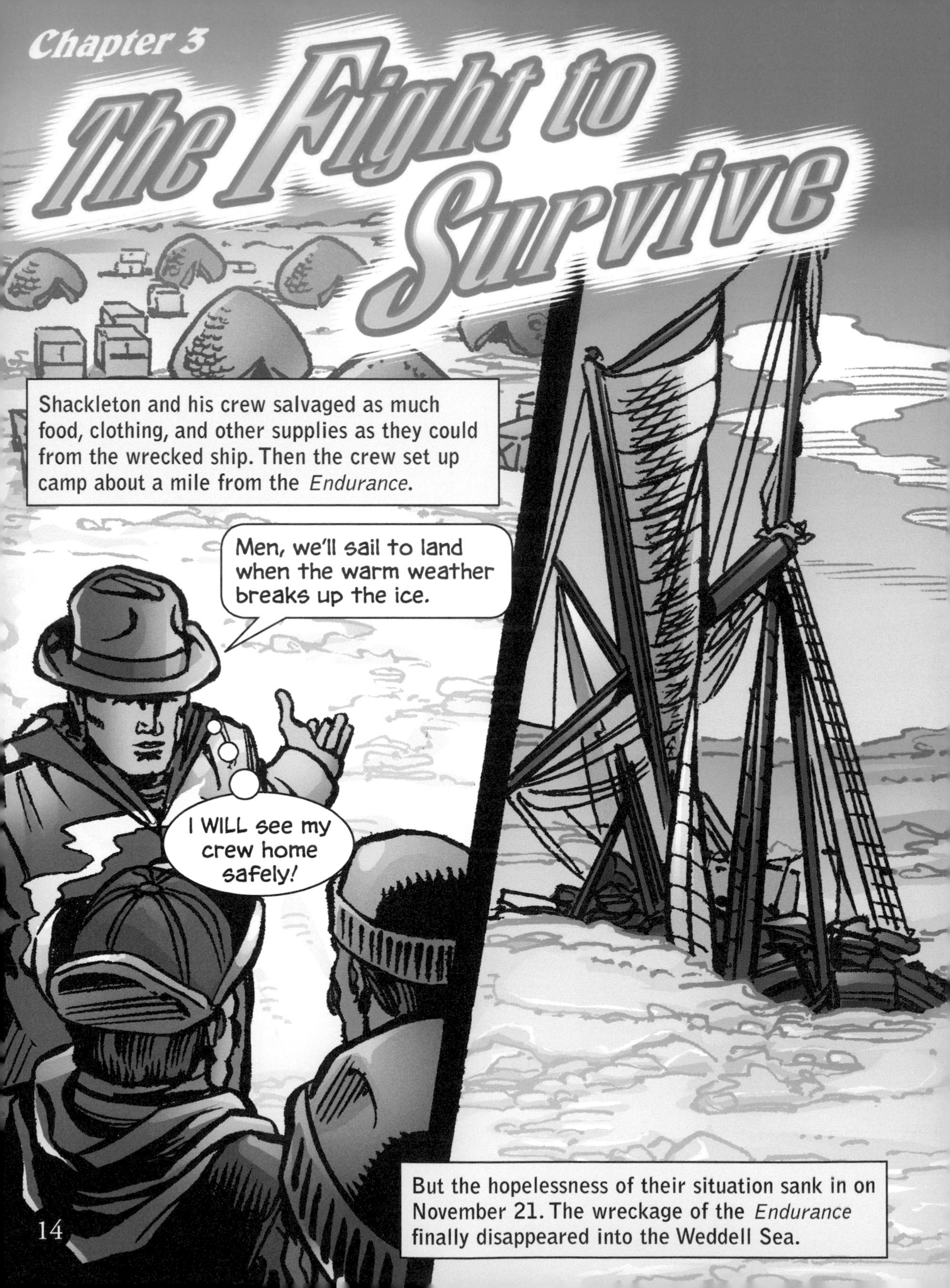
Shackleton and his crew salvaged as much food, clothing, and other supplies as they could from the wrecked ship. Then the crew set up camp about a mile from the *Endurance*.
Men, we'll sail to land when the warm weather breaks up the ice.
I WILL see my crew home safely!
But the hopelessness of their situation sank in on November 21. The wreckage of the *Endurance* finally disappeared into the Weddell Sea.

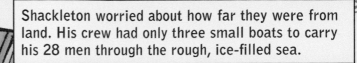

Shackleton worried about how far they were from land. His crew had only three small boats to carry his 28 men through the rough, ice-filled sea.

We are now 250 miles from Paulet Island.

I know there's food stored on the island. It was left years ago by another expedition.

The closer we can get the boats to the island when the ice breaks up, the better off we'll be.

A spell of hard work would do everybody good.

17

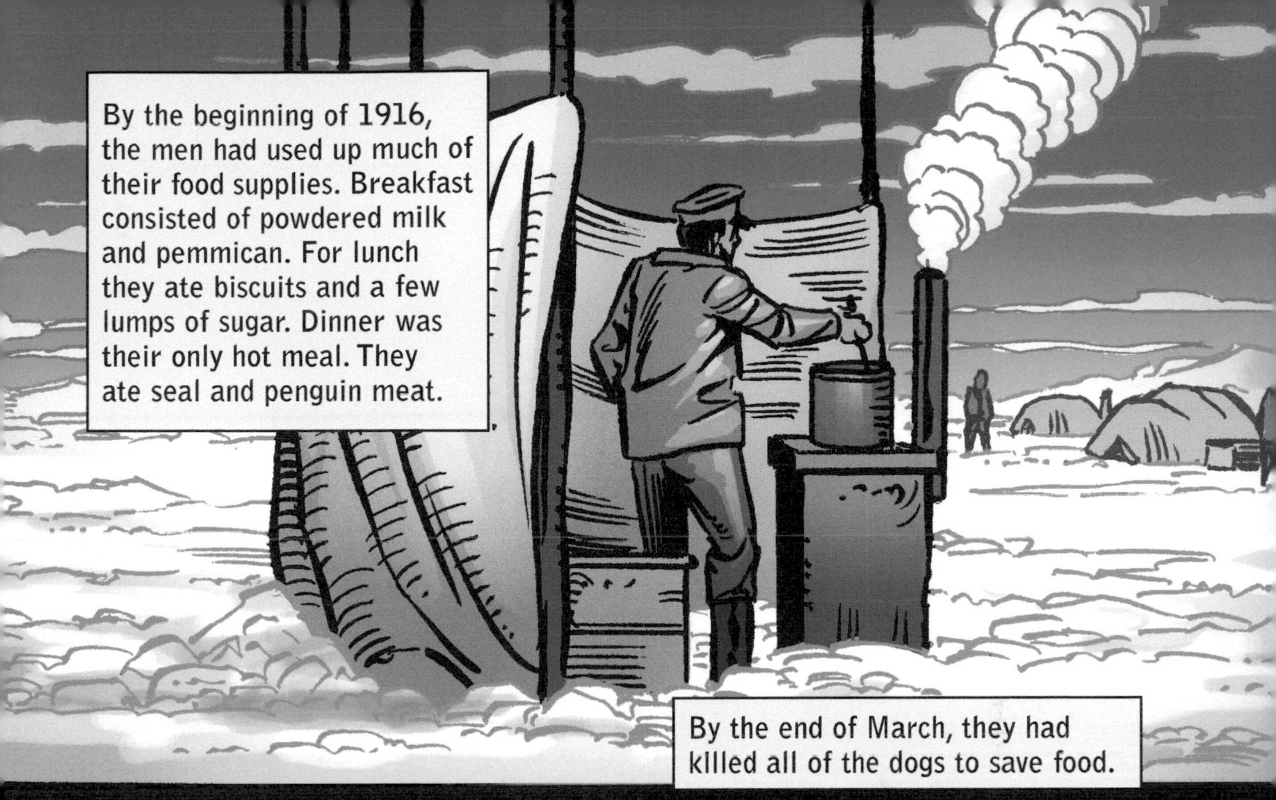
By the beginning of 1916, the men had used up much of their food supplies. Breakfast consisted of powdered milk and pemmican. For lunch they ate biscuits and a few lumps of sugar. Dinner was their only hot meal. They ate seal and penguin meat.
By the end of March, they had killed all of the dogs to save food.

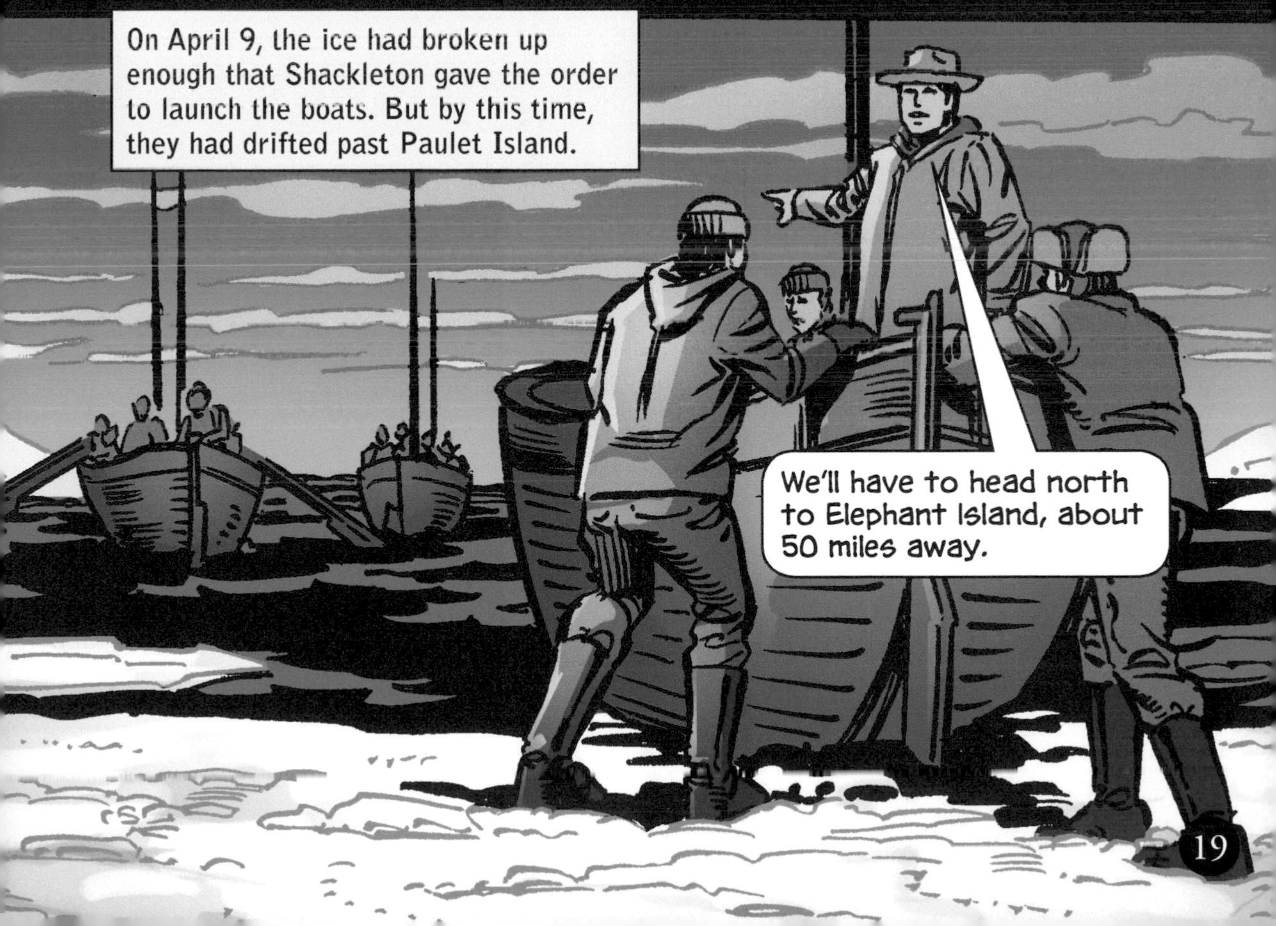
On April 9, the ice had broken up enough that Shackleton gave the order to launch the boats. But by this time, they had drifted past Paulet Island.
We'll have to head north to Elephant Island, about 50 miles away.

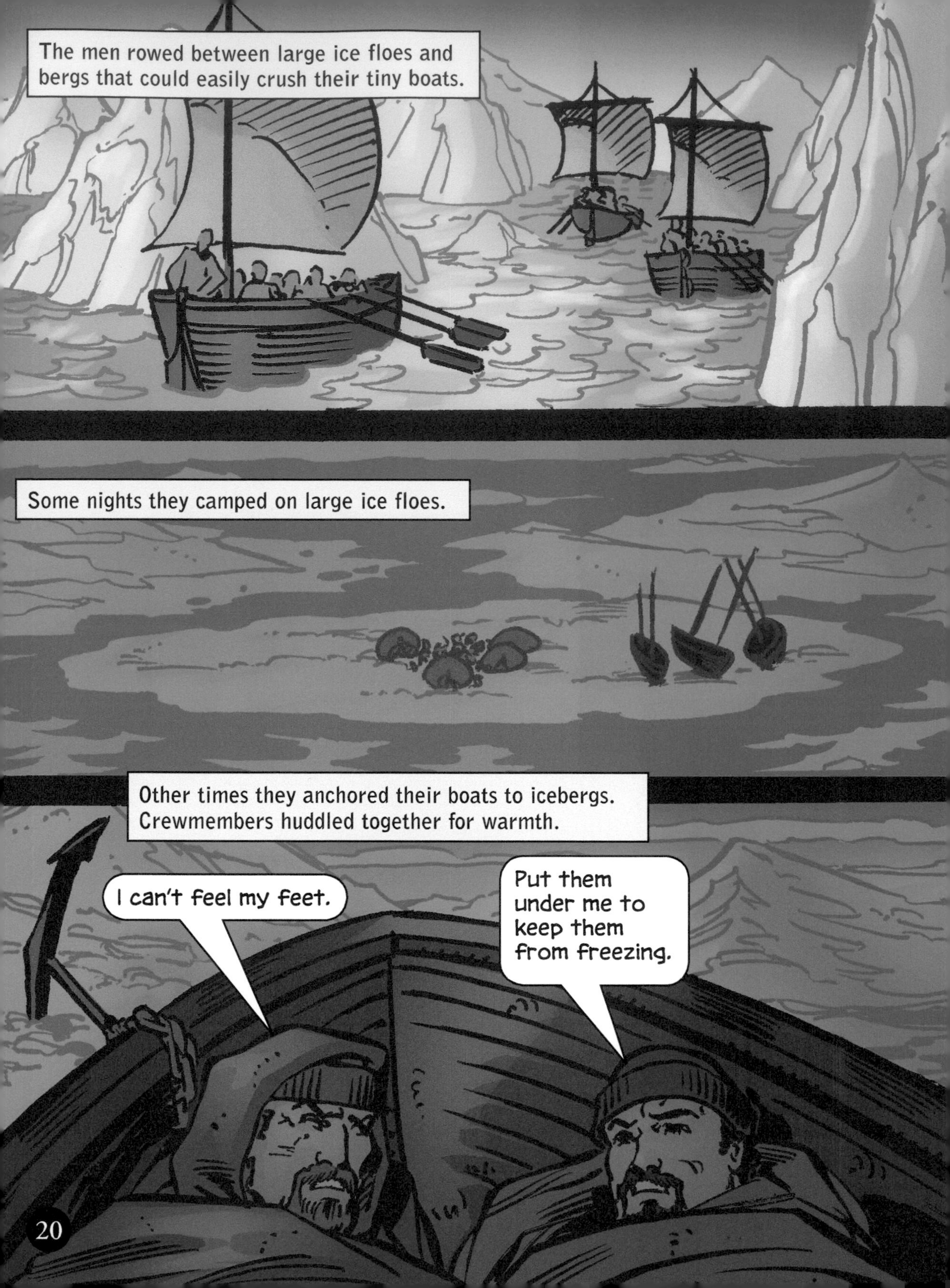

The men rowed between large ice floes and bergs that could easily crush their tiny boats.
Some nights they camped on large ice floes.
Other times they anchored their boats to icebergs. Crewmembers huddled together for warmth.
I can't feel my feet.
Put them under me to keep them from freezing.

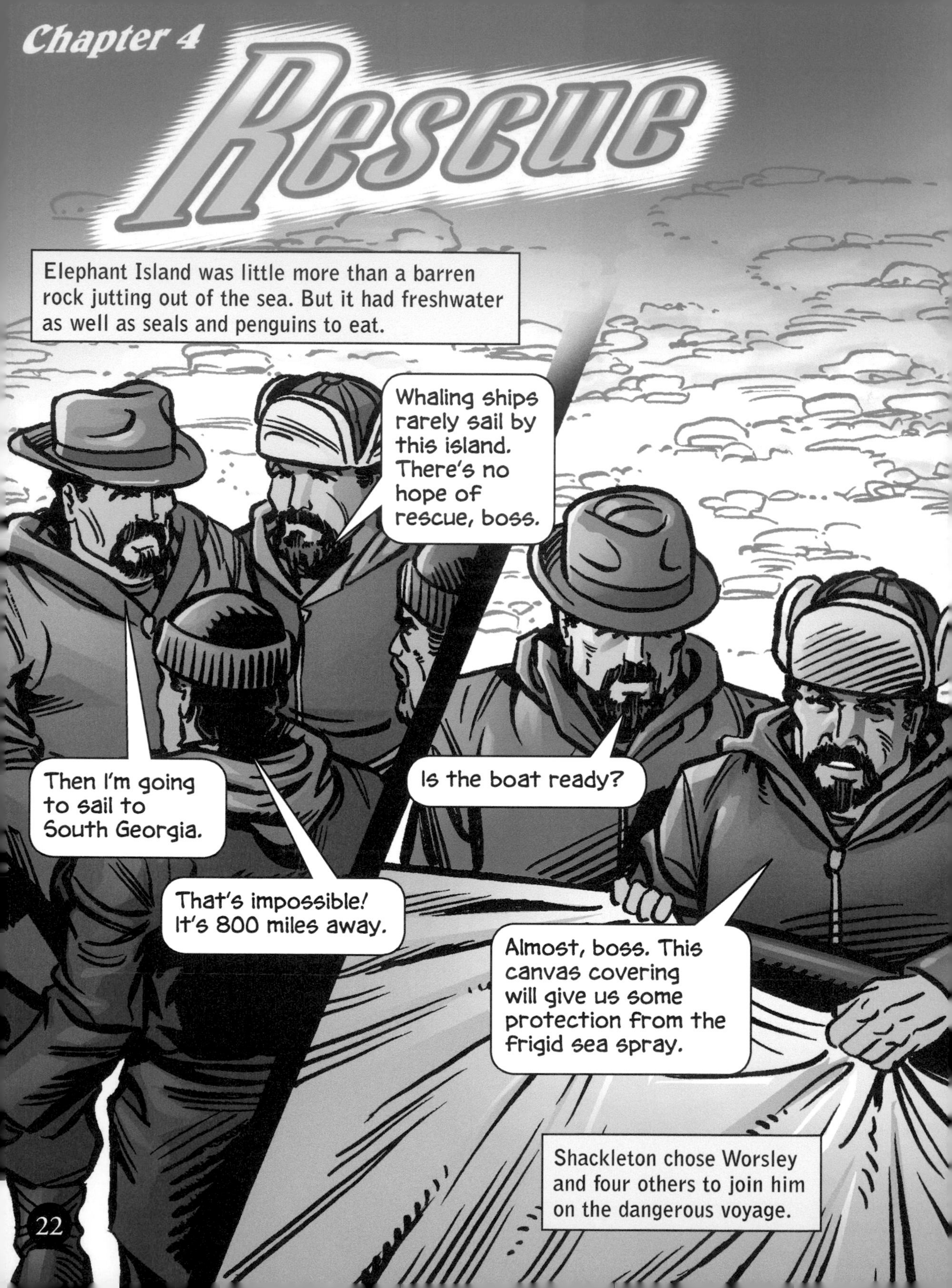
Chapter 4
Rescue
Elephant Island was little more than a barren rock jutting out of the sea. But it had freshwater as well as seals and penguins to eat.
Whaling ships rarely sail by this island. There's no hope of rescue, boss.
Then I'm going to sail to South Georgia.
That's impossible! It's 800 miles away.
Is the boat ready?
Almost, boss. This canvas covering will give us some protection from the frigid sea spray.
Shackleton chose Worsley and four others to join him on the dangerous voyage.

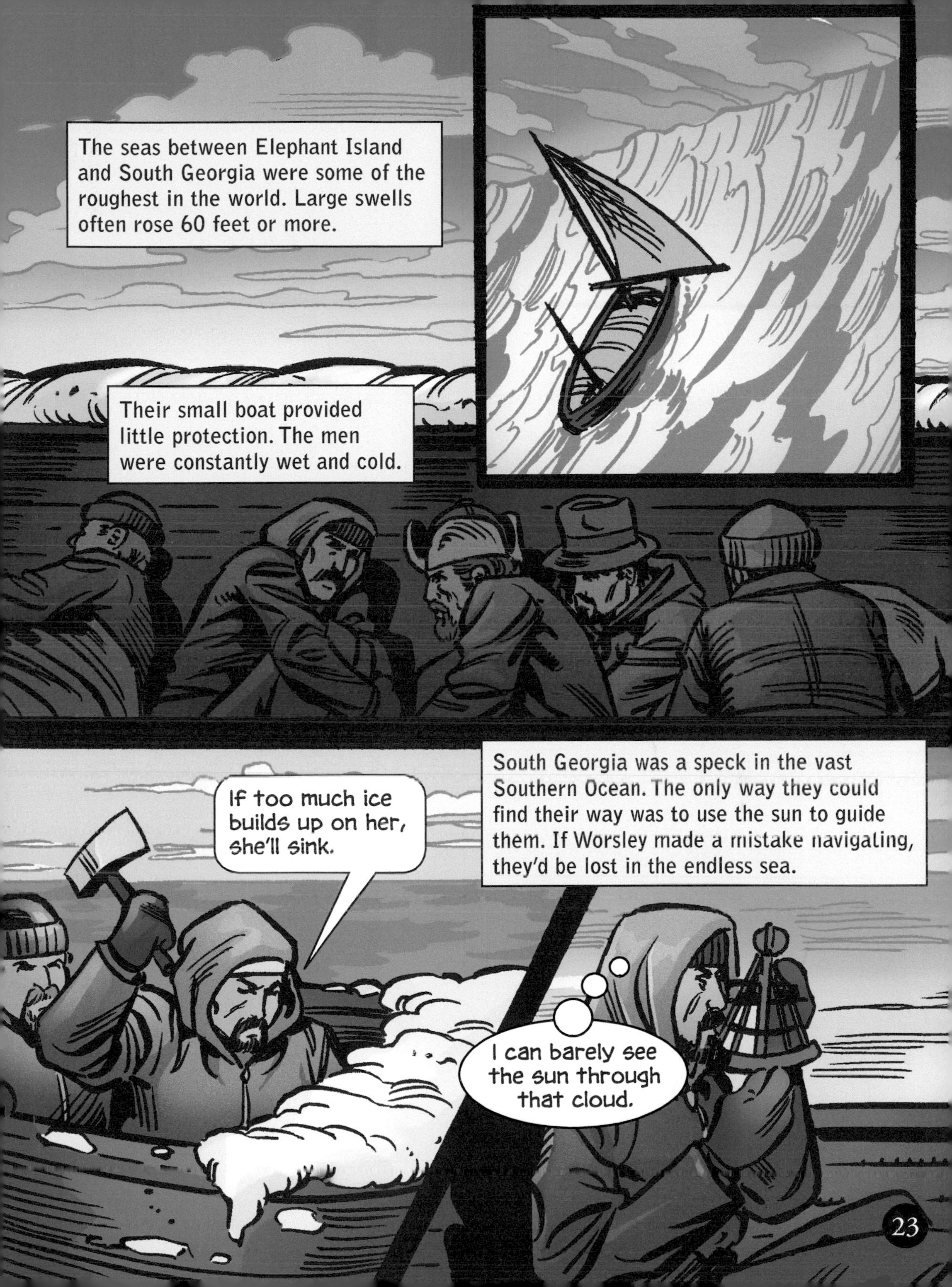
The seas between Elephant Island and South Georgia were some of the roughest in the world. Large swells often rose 60 feet or more.
Their small boat provided little protection. The men were constantly wet and cold.
If too much ice builds up on her, she'll sink.
South Georgia was a speck in the vast Southern Ocean. The only way they could find their way was to use the sun to guide them. If Worsley made a mistake navigating, they'd be lost in the endless sea.
I can barely see the sun through that cloud.

After a 24-day voyage, the men found South Georgia. But one obstacle lay between them and their rescue.

We're on the wrong side of the island.

Then there's no other choice but to climb there.

The boat's lost its rudder, boss. We won't be able to sail around to the whaling station.

He chose Worsley and Thomas Crean to go with him. The other three men were too weak to make the journey.

We'll have to travel more than 20 miles through unexplored mountains.

Read More

Calvert, Patricia. *Sir Ernest Shackleton: By Endurance We Conquer.* Great Explorations. New York: Benchmark Books, 2003.

Currie, Stephen. *Antarctica.* Exploration and Discovery. San Diego: Lucent Books, 2004.

Hooper, Meredith. *Antarctic Adventure: Exploring the Frozen South.* New York: DK, 2000.

White, Matt. *Endurance: Shipwreck and Survival on a Sea of Ice.* Mankato, Minn.: Capstone Curriculum Publishing, 2002.

Bibliography

Alexander, Caroline. *The* Endurance*: Shackleton's Legendary Antarctic Expedition.* New York: Alfred E. Knopf, 1998.

Lansing, Alfred. *Endurance: Shackleton's Incredible Voyage.* Wheaton, Ill.: Tyndale House, 1999.

Shackleton, Ernest. *South: A Memoir of the* Endurance *Voyage.* New York: Carroll & Graf, 1998.

Index